# BURJ KHALIFA

## Kaite Goldsworthy

www.av2books.com

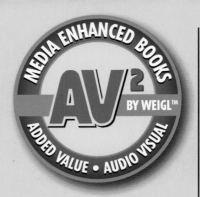

Go to **www.av2books.com**, and enter this book's unique code.

## BOOK CODE

**T246700**

**AV² by Weigl** brings you media enhanced books that support active learning.

AV² provides enriched content that supplements and complements this boo Weigl's AV² books strive to create inspired learning and engage young min in a total learning experience.

## Your AV² Media Enhanced books come alive with...

**Audio**
Listen to sections of the book read aloud.

**Key Words**
Study vocabulary, and complete a matching word activity.

**Video**
Watch informative video clips.

**Quizzes**
Test your knowledge.

**Embedded Weblinks**
Gain additional information for research.

**Slide Show**
View images and captions, and prepare a presentation.

**Try This!**
Complete activities and hands-on experiments.

**... and much, much more**

Published by AV² by Weigl
350 5th Avenue, 59th Floor
New York, NY 10118

Website: www.av2books.com    www.weigl.com

Library of Congress Cataloging-in-Publication Data

Goldsworthy, Kaite.
 Burj Khalifa / Kaite Goldsworthy.
    p. cm. --  (Virtual field trip)
Includes index.
ISBN 978-1-61913-252-8 (hardcover : alk. paper) -- ISBN 978-1-61913-258-0 (softcover : alk. paper)
1.  Burj Khalifa (Dubai, United Arab Emirates)--Juvenile literature.  I. Title.
NA6234.U52D833 2012
725'.2095357--dc22

                        2011045450

Printed in the United States of America in North Mankato, Minnesota
1 2 3 4 5 6 7 8 9 0  16 15 14 13 12

012012
WEP060112

Senior Editor: Heather Kissock
Art Director: Terry Paulhus

Every reasonable effort has been made to trace ownership and to obtain permission to reprint copyright material. The publishers would be pleased to have any errors or omissions brought to their attention so that they may be corrected in subsequent printings.

Weigl acknowledges Getty Images as its primary image supplier for this title.

# Contents

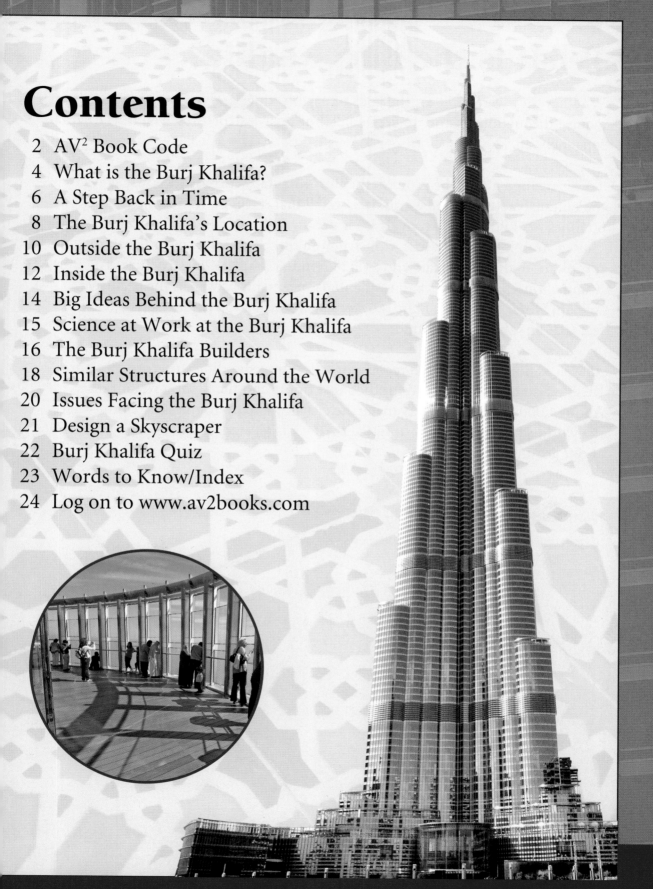

# What is the Burj Khalifa?

Whether they were built for the gods or earthly kings and queens, there has been a quest throughout history to create tall, impressive structures. The Burj Khalifa tops them all.

Towering high above the ground, the Burj Khalifa is currently known as the tallest structure in the world. It is so tall that it can be seen from as far as 60 miles (97 kilometers) away. It is located in Dubai, a city and **emirate** in the United Arab Emirates (UAE). Construction on the massive tower began in 2004. It took more than five years and $1.5 billion to complete the structure. The Burj Khalifa houses businesses and residential apartments as well as the exclusive Armani Hotel. It is more than 160 stories tall, with a top floor that is 2,038 feet (621 m) above the ground.

As well as holding the world record for tallest free-standing structure, the Burj Khalifa also holds the record for the most floors and the highest restaurant. About 4,000 visitors each day make the elevator trip up to the 124th floor, where the world's highest outdoor observation deck is located. It is 1,483 feet (452 m) above ground.

The Burj Khalifa was originally named the Burj Dubai. Its name was changed in honor of Sheik Khalifa bin Zayed al-Nahayan, who provided funding for the project. *Burj* means "tower" in Arabic.

# Snapshot of the UAE

The UAE is a **federation** of seven emirates. These emirates are Dubai, Abu Dhabi, Sharjah, Ajman, Fujairah, Umm al-Qaiwain, and Ras al-Khaimah. Each emirate is governed by its own ruler, with a president responsible for the federation itself. The UAE is located on the Persian Gulf, along the east coast of the Arabian Peninsula.

## INTRODUCING THE UAE

**CAPITAL:** Abu Dhabi

**FLAG:**

**POPULATION:** 5,148,664 (2011)

**OFFICIAL LANGUAGE:** Arabic

**CURRENCY:** Arab Emirate Dirham (AED)

**CLIMATE:** Hot and arid desert climate, with little rainfall

**SUMMER TEMPERATURE:** 90° to 105° Fahrenheit (32° to 41° Celsius)

**WINTER TEMPERATURE:** 73° to 95° F (23° to 35° C)

**TIME ZONE:** Gulf Standard Time (GST)

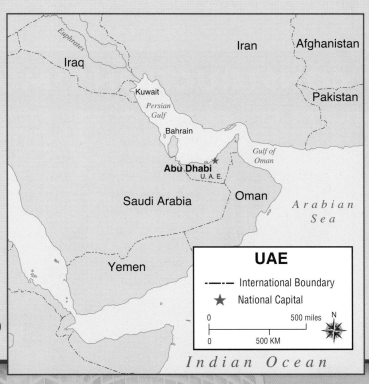

## Arabic Words to Know

As a visitor to a foreign land, it is always important to learn some common words and phrases in the local language. Practice the following phrases before your visit to the UAE.

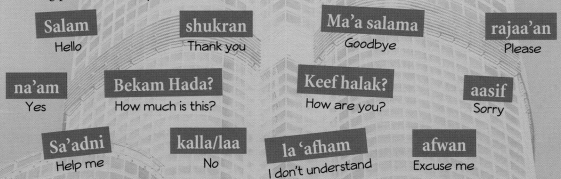

Salam — Hello

shukran — Thank you

Ma'a salama — Goodbye

rajaa'an — Please

na'am — Yes

Bekam Hada? — How much is this?

Keef halak? — How are you?

aasif — Sorry

Sa'adni — Help me

kalla/laa — No

la 'afham — I don't understand

afwan — Excuse me

# A Step Back in Time

Dubai is known for its oil reserves. The oil industry brought business to Dubai from around the world. This improved its economy. Knowing the oil reserves would one day run out, the government wanted to find other ways to support Dubai. Over the last 30 years, progress has been made to transform Dubai into an international tourism **destination**. The Burj Khalifa was built to draw more visitors to the city. Its status as the world's tallest building was to help increase awareness of Dubai around the world.

# CONSTRUCTION TIMELINE

**January 2004**
Excavation on the new building begins.

**February 2004**
Piling begins. When complete, 192 concrete and steel reinforced piles are buried 164 feet (50 m) in the ground to support the building.

**March 2005**
Work on the structure begins. The building starts the climb upwards.

**July 2007**
Level 141 is completed. Even though it is not yet complete, the Burj Khalifa is already the world's tallest building.

In total, building the Burj Khalifa used more than 22 million hours of manpower. During busy days, as many as 12,000 workers were on site.

BURJ DUBAI

The Burj Khalifa was designed by Emaar, a **land development** company in the UAE. The Burj Khalifa has been one of its most important projects. The company's vision was to create a tower that would not only break records, but also be an inspiring symbol of Dubai's progress.

Thirty different companies from around the world worked on site to build the Burj Khalifa.

### September 2007
Level 150 is completed. The tower is now the world's tallest **free-standing** structure.

### April 2008
Level 160 is completed. At this level, the Burj Khalifa is the tallest humanmade structure in the world.

### January 2009
The **spire** is completed, and the Burj Khalifa reaches its final height.

### September 2009
The exterior **cladding** of the tower is finished. It took more than 380 engineers and technicians more than two years to install it.

### January 2010
The tower is officially opened with a ceremony and display of more than 10,000 fireworks. The name is now officially the Burj Khalifa.

The Burj Khalifa became the world's tallest free-standing structure 1,325 days after excavation began.

A laser light show was part of the Burj Khalifa's opening ceremonies.

# The Burj Khalifa's Location

The Burj Khalifa is the centerpiece of a 0.77 square mile (2 square km) area called Downtown Dubai. Downtown Dubai was built by Emaar at a cost of more than $20 billion. It features a number of hotels, shops, and restaurants as well as office buildings and apartments. The Dubai Mall has more than 1,200 different shops as well as a skating rink and an aquarium. Burj Khalifa Lake is home to the Dubai Fountain. With a length of more than two football fields, the fountain features about 6,600 lights as well as jets that shoot water at least 500 feet (152 m) high, all moving in time to classical Arabic music.

The beam of light that shines up to sky from the Dubai Fountain can be seen from more than 20 miles (32 km) away. It is so bright that it can even be seen from space.

# The Burj Khalifa Today

The Burj Khalifa is considered by many to be an incredible feat of construction and **engineering**. From the **foundation** to the spire, every aspect of the tower was carefully designed and executed.

**more than 700 feet (213 m)**

**Spire** The spire at the top of the Burj Khalifa is more than 700 feet (213 m) tall.

**Height** The height of the Burj Khalifa is 2,717 feet (828 m).

**2,717 feet (828 m)**

**Floor Area** The Burj Khalifa has a total floor area of about 3.3 million square feet (306,570 sq. m).

# Outside the Burj Khalifa

*In addition to its record-breaking height, the Burj Khalifa has a number of other remarkable features. Some are not as visible as others, but all play an important role in the design, structure, and function of the tower.*

**Foundation** Though it cannot be seen, the foundation of the Burj Khalifa is a large **reinforced concrete** mat. The mat is more than 12 feet (3.7 m) thick and is supported by concrete piles. It was designed to withstand earthquake activity and any chemicals present in the ground that may cause **erosion**.

It took four separate pours of 441,433 cubic feet (12,500 cubic meters) of concrete to create the mat.

Although the three entrances are at ground level, each one leads to a different floor level inside the podium.

**Podium** The podium serves as the base for the Burj Khalifa. It secures the tower to the ground. Entrances to the tower are located on three sides of the podium. This includes separate entrances for the residences, businesses, and Armani Hotel.

**Layout** The Y-shaped layout allows the building to have three **wings**. The tower rises in tube-like sections above each wing. Some sections end, while others continue to rise. This makes the tower seem to spiral upward. It also allows the building to become narrower as it gets taller.

The tower sections of the Burj Khalifa stop at 26 different levels.

**Spire** The **telescopic** spire at the top of the Burj Khalifa is made from 4,000 tons (3,630 metric tons) of steel. It was built inside the building and raised into position with a **hydraulic** pump. The spire contains equipment for broadcasting and communication.

The top of the spire can sway up to 5 feet (1.5 m) in the wind.

If all the window washing units were put to work at the same time, it would still take up to four months to clean the exterior of the Burj Khalifa.

**Window Washing Bays** With so many windows to keep clean, it is no surprise that the Burj Khalifa has special equipment installed to wash them all. There are 18 window washing units permanently housed in special bays throughout the tower. The machines run on a track to keep the exterior of the building clean.

**Exterior Cladding** The Burj Khalifa has a reflective outer layer of glass, aluminum, and stainless steel. Nearly 26,000 hand-cut glass panels were used. The cladding is designed to withstand the extreme Dubai temperatures. Three hundred specialists were brought in from China to install the cladding.

# VIRTUAL TOUR

The "At The Top" tour to the Burj Khalifa's observation deck is open Sunday to Wednesday from 10:00 a.m. to 10:00 p.m. and Thursday to Saturday from 10:00 a.m. until midnight. The tour leaves from the Dubai Mall and lasts about an hour.

The wall of glass covering the Burj Khalifa is equal in size to 25 American football fields.

# Inside the Burj Khalifa

*The interior of the Burj Khalifa is quite literally a combination of art and science.*

**Interiors** The design inside the Burj Khalifa was inspired by the culture of the area. There are stone floors and handmade rugs as well as glass, stainless steel, and exotic local woods. More than 1,000 pieces of art, many specially created for the Burj Khalifa, are displayed throughout the tower. Works from the Middle East and around the world were chosen to represent Dubai's new role as an international destination.

Many of the colors and shapes used inside the Burj Khalifa complex were inspired by the sands of the nearby Arabian Desert and the curves of Arabic writing.

No elevator in the Burj Kahlifa travels to all of the floors. People must change elevators at a sky lobby to get to the top of the building.

**Elevators** The Burj Khalifa has 57 elevators. Like most tall buildings with many floors, the Burj Khalifa has express elevators that only stop on certain floors to shorten travel time. These floors are known as "sky lobbies." On these floors, guests can change from one elevator to another. The Burj Khalifa has sky lobbies on the 43rd, 76th, and 123rd floors.

**Observation Deck** No visit to the Burj Khalifa would be complete without a trip to the observation deck on the 124th floor. The elevator ride up takes less than 60 seconds. The high-speed, two-floor elevator moves 33 feet (10 m) per second. Upon arrival at the observation deck, there is 360-degree view through the floor-to-ceiling windows. There is also an open-air terrace, the only one in the world at this height.

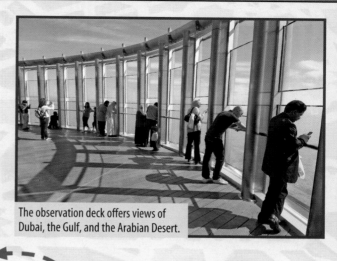
The observation deck offers views of Dubai, the Gulf, and the Arabian Desert.

The Armani Hotel also features its own restaurants. There are eight restaurants in the hotel.

**World's Highest Restaurant** The At.mosphere Restaurant is located on Level 122 of the Burj Khalifa. It offers guests the chance to eat dinner and enjoy incredible views 1,450 feet (442 m) above the ground.

**Apartments and Offices** There are 900 apartments in the Burj Khalifa. The highest apartment is on the 108th floor. The top 37 floors of the tower are office space for businesses. A private express elevator takes business passengers directly to a separate lobby on the 123rd floor.

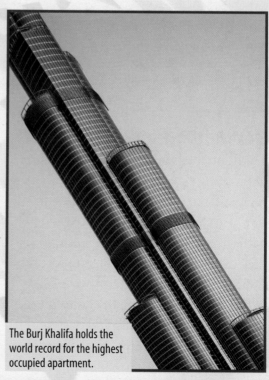
The Burj Khalifa holds the world record for the highest occupied apartment.

# Big Ideas Behind the Burj Khalifa

Building the Burj Khalifa required careful design, planning, and hard work. The builders made great efforts to include elements of Arabic culture in the Burj Khalifa's design.

Spider lilies are found throughout Dubai and the Gulf area.

## Floor Plan

The design for the Y-shaped floor plan of the Burj Khalifa came from an unlikely source, a desert flower. The plan was inspired by the spider lily. This flower grows throughout the UAE. The Burj Khalifa was designed with a central core and three wings built away from it. Similarly, the long thin petals of the spider lily extend from the center of the flower. The "Y" shape of the building adds stability and helps to reduce the effect of the wind, while providing spectacular views.

## Geometric Patterning

Traditional **Islamic** art and architecture often feature **geometric** patterns. Shapes such as circles, squares, triangles, and stars are combined and repeated. These patterns are seen as spiritual because they can be infinite, or going on forever. Traditional Islamic patterns were used in the Burj Khalifa. The tower itself was designed in an upward spiral pattern, which symbolizes going toward heaven in traditional Islamic architecture.

Although geometric patterns are commonly found in Islamic architecture, they were also used by ancient Greeks and Romans.

# Science at Work at the Burj Khalifa

Building any structure has it challenges. Constructing the world's tallest building presented some unique ones.

The hexagonal-shaped core of the Burj Khalifa helps it withstand winds and earthquakes.

## Central Core

A specially reinforced concrete core makes the Burj Khalifa much stronger than buildings built with a steel frame. This is known as a "**buttressed** core." The center of a building with a buttressed core is solid, with concrete walls attached to it. The walls of each of the three wings slope away from the core. The buttressed core helps to reduce torque. This is the force that causes objects to turn or rotate. The buttressed core makes the tower more stable.

## Setbacks

When building a skyscraper so tall, one of the biggest challenges is weight. The taller a building is, the more weight the base of the building must support. A wider base can support a taller building, such as a pyramid. The Burj Khalifa is built using this idea in a slightly different way. As the building spirals upward, the width of the tower changes with steps or ledges inward. These are called "setbacks." Each setback allows the tower to get thinner as it gets taller. These setbacks also help with wind **resistance**. This is another challenge tall buildings face.

The setbacks break up the wind, causing it to hit the building with less force.

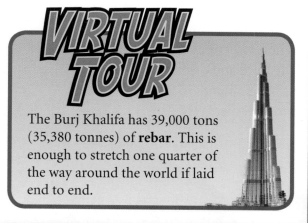

## VIRTUAL TOUR

The Burj Khalifa has 39,000 tons (35,380 tonnes) of **rebar**. This is enough to stretch one quarter of the way around the world if laid end to end.

# The Burj Khalifa Builders

Designing and building the Burj Khalifa was the responsibility of a team of professionals who had worked on some of the tallest buildings in world.

The Trump International Hotel and Tower shares many features with the Burj Khalifa.

### Adrian Smith Architect

American architect Adrian Smith is one of the most well-known architects in the world. He was a design partner at Skidmore, Owings & Merrill (SOM), the architecture and engineering firm that was awarded the job of designing the Burj Khalifa. Smith also designed the Jin Mao Tower in Shanghai and the Trump International Hotel and Tower in Chicago. These structures are the third and twelfth tallest buildings in the world respectively.

### William F. Baker
**Structural Engineer**

Bill Baker was the head structural engineer at SOM. The Trump International Hotel and Tower and the 1,820-foot (555-m) Lotte Tower in Seoul, Korea, are just two of the buildings he has helped create. To safely build the Burj Khalifa so high, Baker invented the buttressed core that is used at the center of the tower.

Bill Baker and his team worked on China's Zifeng Tower, ranked as one of the world's 10 highest buildings.

### Mohamed Alabbar
**Chairman of Emaar Properties**

Mohamed Alabbar had the vision to build the Burj Khalifa. He wanted the tower to represent the union of Arabia and the rest of world. He also wanted the Burj Khalifa to bring the art of design and the science of engineering together.

Mohamed Alabbar wanted the Burj Khalifa to show the world what Dubai and the United Arab Emirates were able to do.

## Architects

An architect designs all types of buildings, from family homes and apartments to schools, airports, hospitals, and high rises. Architects plan how a building will look and function to meet the needs of the people who will use it. They are also responsible for making it safe. As well as planning a high rise, Adrian Smith and his team had to design the Burj Khalifa for many different uses, including business and residential.

Architects use both mathematics and science in planning and designing buildings.

## Engineers

Engineers play a key role in construction planning. Before construction begins, an engineer takes the plans for a structure and analyzes how it can be built. For example, structural engineers study the weight of a structure. Using computers, they plan beams, floors, and other framework to allow for the load to be safely distributed. Structural engineers carry out inspections at different stages of the process to make sure the structure will be safe, strong, and stable.

Structural engineers design everything from bridges and buildings to boats and aircraft.

## Ironworkers

An ironworker assembles the metal framework used in constructing buildings. Ironworkers follow the plans created by the architect and structural engineer. They cut and **weld** metal beams and columns as well as operate cranes and heavy machinery to put the beams in place. The Burj Khalifa features ironwork over entranceways as well as within the building.

Being an ironworker can be a challenging and sometimes dangerous job.

# Similar Structures Around the World

A skyscraper is defined as a building that rises above a city's skyline, giving it a distinctive appearance. Skyscrapers can be found in many parts of the world. Wherever they are found, they contribute to the city in which they stand and become landmarks in their own right.

## CN Tower

**BUILT:** 1976
**LOCATION:** Toronto, Canada
**DESIGN:** John Andrews and Webb, Zerafa, Menkes, Housden Architects
**DESCRIPTION:** The CN Tower is a traditional tower, with less than half of the floor space considered usable. It was built by the Canadian National Railway to send radio and TV signals. Before the Burj Khalifa was built, the CN Tower held the record as the tallest free-standing building. It stands at 1,815 feet (553 m).

Taipei 101 is designed to withstand earthquake tremors and typhoons. It is considered one of the most stable buildings ever built.

The CN Tower allows visitors to wear a harness and take an "Edge Walk" on a ledge 116 stories above the ground.

## Taipei 101

**BUILT:** 2004
**LOCATION:** Taipei, Taiwan
**DESIGN:** C.Y. Lee & Partners
**DESCRIPTION:** Taipei 101 has 101 floors above ground and 5 below. It was designed using modern technology and traditional Asian architecture and symbols. The tower has the appearance of a modern day **pagoda** and is about 1,671 feet (510 m) tall.

## Petronas Towers

**BUILT:** 1998
**LOCATION:** Kuala Lumpur, Malaysia
**DESIGN:** Cesar Pelli & Associates
**DESCRIPTION:** The Petronas Towers were designed to be a modern reflection of the Islamic history and culture of Malaysia. They are built from high-strength concrete to reduce swaying. Each building has a concrete core with an exterior wall of glass and stainless steel. At 1,483 feet (452 m), the Petronas Towers are the tallest twin towers in the world.

The two identical towers are connected by a bridge on the 41st floor.

The Willis Tower was the world's tallest building for 25 years, until the Petronas Towers were built. It remains the tallest building in the United States.

## Willis (Sears) Tower

**BUILT:** 1973
**LOCATION:** Chicago, Illinois, United States
**DESIGN:** Skidmore, Owings & Merrill
**DESCRIPTION:** The 1,450-foot (442-m) tower was originally built for Sears, Roebuck & Co. It was designed to be one of the world's tallest buildings. The building was created as nine separate square towers which all rose to the 50th floor. After the 50th floor, the towers were staggered, with the final two towers rising to the 110th floor. This gave the building its unique appearance.

# Issues Facing the Burj Khalifa

The Burj Khalifa is still a very young building. It was built with the latest technology and construction materials so that it would last. Great care was taken to select materials that would age well in a hot and harsh environment.

## WHAT IS THE ISSUE?

The climate and soil conditions in Dubai can cause problems for the materials used to construct a building.

A building the size of the Burj Khalifa requires a great deal of energy for lighting and power.

## EFFECTS

Chemicals in groundwater can cause the concrete foundation to **corrode**. Hot, dry conditions may affect the life span of the glazed cladding, causing it to crack.

The costs of running such an enormous building can be great, both financially and environmentally.

## ACTION TAKEN

Checking the foundations and cladding regularly and making repairs when necessary keeps the building in good condition.

**Condensation** from inside the building's air conditioning system is recycled. It is collected and used to water the landscaped gardens around the building.

# Design a Skyscraper

A skyscraper is being built in your honor, and you get to be the architect to design it. Before you begin, there are many things to take into account. Where will it be located? Who will use it? How will its design reflect you and your personality? Will the building blend in with its surroundings or stand out? Is your building located somewhere that will require special designs or materials to accommodate severe or unusual weather? Will it have special features, such as solar panels, to make it environmentally responsible?

## Materials
- paper (both blank and graph paper would be best)
- sharp pencil
- eraser
- hard, flat surface
- ruler

## Instructions

1. Brainstorm your building design. Architects often draw up many different design ideas before the final one is chosen. Draw up rough basic sketches of your ideas before selecting one.

2. When you have chosen your design, draw it out on graph paper. Be sure to include important dimensions, such as height and width, on your plan. Use your ruler to draw out your design.

3. Be sure to add details such as windows and doors. If your building has any special architectural details, such as arches, columns, moldings, or other features, be sure to include them.

When you are finished, look at your design. Take the approach of a structural engineer. Do you think it could be safely built? Do you see anything you would change?

# Burj Khalifa Quiz

**Q** How tall is the Burj Khalifa?

**A** 2,717 feet (828 m)

**Q** What is the name of the plant that inspired the Burj Khalifa's design?

**A** The spider lily

**Q** What was the original name of the Burj Khalifa?

**A** Burj Dubai.

**Q** What is special about the elevator to the observation deck?

**A** It moves 33 feet (10 m) every second. It also has two floors.

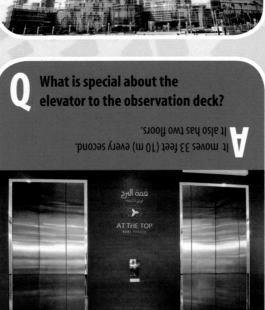

# Words to Know

**buttressed:** built against a wall for support

**cladding:** a protective covering or coating

**condensation:** when a gas or vapor becomes a liquid

**corrode:** to destroy a metal through chemical action

**destination:** a place to go

**emirate:** a nation ruled by an emir, a prince or chief in the Middle East

**engineering:** using science and math to design and manufacture machines, structures, and processes

**erosion:** the wearing away of rocks, soil, etc., by the action of water, ice, or wind

**excavation:** digging a hole

**federation:** the joining together of several states to form a political union

**foundation:** the base for something

**free-standing:** not attached or supported by another object

**geometric:** characterized by regular lines and shapes

**hydraulic:** operated by fluid that is under pressure

**Islamic:** relating to the religion of Islam

**land development:** converting raw land into residential, commercial, or industrial building sites

**pagoda:** a religious building of the Far East

**piling:** driving metal bars into a foundation to make it stronger

**rebar:** a steel bar put into concrete to make it stronger

**reinforced concrete:** a building material that has steel bars placed in it

**resistance:** a force that opposes or stops

**spire:** a tapering, conical structure on top of a building

**telescopic:** capable of seeing distant objects

**weld:** to join metals by applying heat

**wings:** structures attached to and connected internally with the side of a main building

# Index

# Log on to www.av2books.com

AV² by Weigl brings you media enhanced books that support active learning. Go to www.av2books.com, and enter the special code found on page 2 of this book. You will gain access to enriched and enhanced content that supplements and complements this book. Content includes video, audio, weblinks, quizzes, a slide show, and activities.

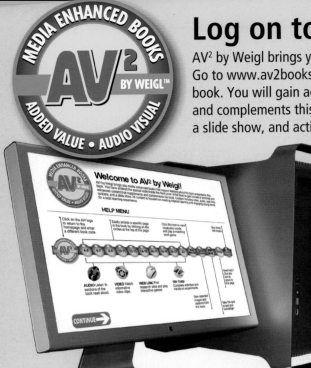

## Audio
Listen to sections of the book read aloud.

## Video
Watch informative video clips.

## Embedded Weblinks
Gain additional information for research.

## Try This!
Complete activities and hands-on experiments.

# WHAT'S ONLINE?

|  Try This! |  Embedded Weblinks |  Video | EXTRA FEATURES |
|---|---|---|---|
| Identify the features of the Burj Khalifa. | Find out more about the Burj Khalifa. | Watch a video that celebrates the official opening of the Burj Khalifa. |  **Audio** Listen to sections of the book read aloud. |
| Imagine that you are designing the Burj Khalifa. | Compare the Burj Khalifa to other towers in the world. | Watch a video to see what it was like to be a construction worker on the Burj Khalifa. |  **Key Words** Study vocabulary, and complete a matching word activity. |
| Test your knowledge of the Burj Khalifa. | Visit a museum devoted to skyscrapers. | See how the Burj Khalifa was constructed. |  **Slide Show** View images and capti⊘ and prepare a presenta⊘ |
| | | |  **Quizzes** Test your knowledge. |

**AV² was built to bridge the gap between print and digital. We encourage you to tell us what you like and what you want to see in the future.**

**Sign up to be an AV² Ambassador at www.av2books.com/ambassador.**